Sleeping Giants

A Guide to Earth's Geological Anomalies

Table of Contents

Chapter 1. Introduction

Prepare to embark on a sprawling journey deep below our feet as we unveil the sleeping giants of our planet, those stunning geological anomalies that continue to bewilder and fascinate us to this day. "Sleeping Giants: A Guide to Earth's Geological Anomalies" takes you on an engaging exploration through the world's most incredible geological marvels—towering mountains, majestic canyons, mysterious caves, and so much more. Although taking up a scientific lens, this Special Report is crafted in a truly accessible and enjoyable style, making the complex wonders of geology feel as homely as your own backyard. Richly detailed yet wonderfully readable, it invites you on an adventure, one you can embark on from the comfort of your living room. So, pull up a chair, immersity yourself in our planet's untold sagas, and tap into a wellspring of earthly wonders that promises to inform, inspire, and enthrall.

Chapter 2. Awakening the Giants: A Geological Prelude

The resilience of rock meeting the insatiable curiosity of humankind sparks a story as old as time. With every twist, turn, and precipitous descent into the bowels of the Earth, the tale of our planet's birth, life, and future unravels.

2.1. The Language of the Earth

Quartz, mica, feldspar, and hornblende—the components of granite—are as distinct as poetic verse, each radiating its hue into the amalgam of color belied by the mundane gray of the whole. Understanding the composition and formation of rocks is as essential to the study of our planet as are words to a sentence or melodies to a symphony.

Nearly 4.6 billion years ago, Earth took shape out of the cosmic dust. It soon developed a crust, essentially a veneer, the first layer in what would ultimately become a multi-tiered structure. This crust was composed of crustal rocks, a veritable Rosetta Stone for the geologist seeking to interpret the Earth's history. In reading these rocks, Earth's chronicles of birth, transformation, and renewal become apparent.

2.2. Unfolding the Layers

Beneath our feet yawn vast expanses of the crust, mantle, outer core, and finally, the inner core. The crust, from its oceanic to its continental manifestations, is remarkably varied. The thinnest portion—about 3 miles beneath the ocean—lies in stark contrast to the thickest part, spanning an impressive 43 miles beneath grand mountain ranges.

This mantle extends downwards to about 1,800 miles and is known as the lithosphere. Further below, over 3,000 miles under the surface, resides the Earth's core.

Between the lithosphere and the core, the asthenosphere and mesosphere form transitional zones of unique composition and characteristic, with temperature and pressure increasing dramatically with depth.

2.3. On Shifts and Plates

Plate tectonics, the concept of Earth's lithosphere divided into several pieces moving independently yet interacting across their margins, forms the cornerstone of modern geology. These giant segments move, collide, and grind against one another, causing phenomena like earthquakes, volcanic eruptions, and even the creation of mountain ranges.

It's at these junctures where the lithosphere's saga gets particularly riveting. As two plates converge, one may be forced beneath the other in a process known as subduction. Here, we witness the astonishing sight of one slab of Earth's crust being reintegrated into the mantle.

On the other hand, when two plates diverge, a unique opportunity arises for fresh crust to form — this occurs at the world's oceanic ridges, which are essentially geological conveyer belts delivering new lithosphere.

2.4. Earth's Humble Beginnings

Our planet's earliest epochs, from the Hadean Eon (beginning 4.6 billion years ago) into the Archean Eon (4 billion to 2.5 billion years ago), laid the foundation for the geological marvels we observe today. It was during this time the first primitive continental crust known as cratons formed.

These ancient fragments continue to serve as pilings, upon which continents have grown and reshaped over eons. It's the metamorphism of granite to change into gneiss that tells the tale of our earliest continental buildup under extreme heat and pressure.

2.5. The Power of Water

Completing the relentless sculpting of Earth's face is the power of water. Oceans, rivers, ice—all of them bear gifts of biting erosion and gentle deposition, shaping landscapes and seascapes in their capricious ballet of destruction and creation. Grand canyons, fertile plains, spectacular cliffs, and echoey caves all chronicle the artistry of H2O.

From the glacial striations seen in the U-shaped valleys of the Alps to the alluvial deposits blanketing the fertile plains of the Nile, water has been a mighty and creative natural sculptor.

With hard rock and the persistent movement of water, the foundations of our Earth took shape. This dynamic duo—rock and water—continue to play a central role in the ongoing narrative of our planet, reshaping our environments, spurring evolution, and carving a habitat well suited to support a dazzling array of life-forms.

In the pages to follow, we drive deeper into the marvels shaped by the geological forces beneath our feet. Together, we'll trek over majestic terrains, plunge into the hearts of jewel-like mines, scale the pinnacles of mountains, and plunge into the depths of oceans, where the saga of the Earth—our home—is etched in stone. It's a journey of discovery, each rock, each ripple in a canyon wall, and each crystalline cave formation tells, if one knows how to read it, an extraordinary chapter of our Earth's life story.

Chapter 3. Mountains: The Skyward Sentinels of Earth

A breathtaking sight for all who witness their grandeur, mountains serve as spectacular skyward sentinels of Earth. These magnificent geological features have been inspiring poets, philosophers, and scientists for centuries. Found in every corner of the world, mountains embody the majesty of our planet and stand as key indicators of the dynamic processes that shape the Earth.

3.1. The Birth of Mountains

The story of mountains starts with the inception of the Earth itself, approximately 4.6 billion years ago. But it wasn't until around 3 billion years later, during the Proterozoic Eon, that the earliest mountain-building processes began. This was made possible by plate tectonics, a geological theory that explains the creation, movement, and destruction of the Earth's crust.

According to plate tectonics, the Earth's lithosphere is divided into a number of large and small tectonic plates. These plates move around due to the convective currents generated from the heat of the Earth's mantle and core. When two plates collide—or "converge"—the immense pressure and friction cause the crust to crumple and rise, leading to the formation of mountain ranges. We call this phenomenon orogeny.

An excellent example of orogeny is the formation of the Himalayas. As the Indian Plate collides with the Eurasian Plate, the Earth's crust rises to form this magnificent mountain range. With Mount Everest standing at a staggering 8,848.86 meters, it's a breathtaking testament to the power of tectonic forces.

3.2. Anatomy of a Mountain

On the surface, mountains may just seem like giant hunks of rock. However, their internal structure reveals a far more complex picture.

At the most basic level, mountains are composed of three main components: the core, the mantle, and the crust. However, not all mountain ranges share the same geological blueprints. Let's break down these components.

1. **The Core**: Comprising the innermost layers of a mountain, the core is often composed of the original crustal rocks that predated the mountain-building process. Depending on the mountain region, these rocks could be hundreds of millions to billions of years old.

2. **The Mantle**: Not to be confused with the Earth's mantle, this refers to the middle segment of a mountain's structure. It often contains folded and thrusted rock layers, representing the scars of the mountain's violent birth.

3. **The Crust**: This is the mountain's skin—the exposed layer that we see. It can be composed of a variety of rock types, depending on the geology of the region.

The incredible diversity and complexity of each mountain's structure ultimately contribute to the unique landscape and ecological conditions we find within a specific mountain range.

3.3. Mountains: More Than Just Rock

Mountains are not just collections of stone jutting out from the Earth—they offer an extensive array of biodiversity and rich ecosystems within their slopes, foothills, and valleys. They are home to countless species of animals and plants, many of which are endemic, meaning they are found nowhere else in the world.

The Andean Condor soaring against a backdrop of the majestic Andes peaks, the Snow Leopard camouflaged in the snowy Himalayan terrain, or the endangered Mountain Gorilla dwelling within the heights of the Virunga Mountains in Africa—all these species have adapted to the harsh mountaintop conditions, demonstrating an impressive resilience to the cooler temperatures, less oxygen, and intense ultraviolet radiation at high altitudes.

Furthermore, mountains also play a significant role in influencing our weather and climate. As wind pushes up against the mountain, it cools and condenses, leading to precipitation on the "windward" side. This phenomenon, known as orographic precipitation, often leads to lush, green landscapes. Meanwhile, the "leeward" side of the mountain is usually arid, creating what's known as a rain shadow. This effect is why one can find deserts just beyond high mountains, like the Great Basin Desert east of the Sierra Nevada range.

3.4. Mountains: The Lifeblood of Civilization

Mountains provide countless resources that are pivotal for human survival and development. They feed our rivers, house our forests, offer mineral wealth, and provide habitats for a rich diversity of wildlife. Mountains, hence, stand as more than just geological formations—they are the lifeblood of civilizations, an integral part of human culture and history.

On a tangible level, the fresh, clear water flowing down from the mountaintops provides sustenance for countless communities, cities, and agricultural activities downstream. Metals and minerals mined from mountains have fueled industries and advanced technologies, driving societal progress and economic growth.

On an intangible level, mountains have been ingrained in human lore and spirituality for millennia. They've been considered sacred spaces and dwelling places of the gods in many cultures. From Mount Olympus in Greece to Mount Fuji in Japan and Mount Kailash in Tibet, mountains have often been associated with divine powers or religious reverence and continue to inspire awe and respect.

3.5. The Future of Mountains: A Delicate Balance

Though mountains are symbols of permanence and strength, they are not immune to change. Global warming, deforestation, unregulated tourism, and mining are all taking their toll on these grand structures, threatening not just the biodiversity within their ecosystems, but also the people who rely on them for their livelihoods.

As we march into the future, it's more critical than ever to protect and respect these towering giants. Their story, their structure, their impact, and their significance all serve as a vivid reminder of our complicated relationship with the environment and our responsibility toward its preservation. Thus, mountains will continue their role as the earth's skyward senticels—majestic, compelling, and essential.

From their violent birth through tectonic clashes, through their evolving roles as habitats, climate regulators, resource providers, and religious sanctuaries, to their uncertain future in the face of human activities, the story of mountains is a compelling saga of the Earth itself. Their towering peaks and rugged landscapes are a testament not only to our planet's dynamic nature, but also to the interconnected tapestry of life they support. As guardians of the skyline, they offer us a window into our Earth's past, give us life in the present, and hold valuable lessons for the future.

Chapter 4. Take a Deep Dive: The Mystique of Oceanic Trenches

In the great expanse of the world's oceans, mysterious chasms of plummeting depth nestle in the abyss, cloaked in an enveloping blackness. These are the oceanic trenches—the deepest parts of the oceans, formidable and mysterious, teeming with a cornucopia of life forms both fantastical and awe-inspiring.

4.1. The Formation of Trenches

To begin our deep dive, it's crucial to explore how these submarine canyons form. Our understanding of their origins is relatively recent, stemming from plate tectonic theory developed during the mid-20th century. This theory posits, tremendously simplified, that the Earth's crust is divided into a series of plates. These often-enormous slabs continually move and interact, fostering the creation of many of the Earth's geological features in the process, oceanic trenches included.

When an oceanic plate encounters a continental plate, driven by convection currents within the Earth's mantle, it's forced downward in a process known as subduction. This plunging motion forms a deep, narrow depression—our oceanic trench. Over many millions of years, subduction zones can reach staggering depths and encompass large swathes of oceanic floor.

4.2. Notable Trenches

There are numerous oceanic trenches worldwide. Let's explore some of the most notable ones.

4.2.1. The Mariana Trench

The Mariana Trench earns the title of Earth's deepest oceanic trench, reaching depths of nearly 36,000 feet—truly an abyss. Named after the nearby Mariana Islands, this trench lies in the western Pacific Ocean. With pressure at its deepest point, the Challenger Deep, reaching over 1,000 times the standard atmospheric pressure at sea level, and temperatures between 1 to 4 degrees Celsius, it is a uniquely harsh environment.

4.2.2. The Tonga Trench

Located in the southwestern Pacific Ocean, the Tonga Trench is another significant player. The second-deepest trench on Earth, it reaches depths of over 35,000 feet. While it's richly populated with marine life, this trench, unfortunately, features frequent seismic activity due to subduction of the Pacific Plate beneath the Tonga Plate.

4.2.3. The Peru-Chile Trench

Another site where tectonic plates collide is the Peru-Chile Trench, otherwise known as the Atacama Trench. This trench, named in reference to the two adjacent South American nations, stretches for approximately 5,900 kilometers with a maximum depth of 8,020 meters. Its distinctive marine ecosystems make it a subject of both academic and practical research interest.

4.3. Life in the Trenches: Extremeophiles and More

The crushing pressure, near-freezing temperatures, and dearth of sunlight make trenches seemingly inhospitable. And yet, life perseveres. Many creatures call these trenches home, their bodies uniquely adapted to the challenging conditions.

At these depths, organisms need to withstand the colossal pressure, comparable to having an elephant standing on your thumbnail! Some species, like amphipods and snailfish, have evolved gelatinous bodies that are largely incompressible, thus facilitating survival under such extreme pressures.

Nutrient scarcity is another significant challenge for trench inhabitants. Detritus from the upper ocean layers, often termed 'marine snow,' provides a primary food source. Species such as the Fangtooth fish and the Giant amphipod have evolved to become opportunistic feeders, eating whatever they come across.

Some creatures can even survive without sunlight. Chemical reactions between seawater and rocks, particularly in hydrothermal vent communities, can create sources of energy in a process known as chemosynthesis. These organisms, often various microbes, are coined 'extremophiles,' for their ability to persist under extreme conditions.

4.4. Exploring the Depths: Technology and Discoveries

Delving into the abyss requires technology able to withstand the extreme conditions. Traditional submersibles have limitations due to extreme pressures and poor visibility. Today, remotely operated vehicles (ROVs) carry high-definition cameras and scientific instruments to these depths, controlled by operators on surface vessels.

The list of findings and discoveries is ever-growing. In the Mariana Trench, a handful of expeditions have made it to Challenger Deep. The most recent involved movie director James Cameron, who descended solo in 2012 in the Deepsea Challenger, a collaboration between filmmaking, science, and private enterprise.

In the Tonga Trench, jellyfish-like creatures known as ctenophores were spotted, showing us how life can persist even in the harshest environments. Peru-Chile Trench investigations have rewarded us with better understandings of geological processes and local ecosystems.

In closing, oceanic trenches adorn the seabed like colossal scars, contributing to the rich diversity and intricate complexity of Earth's geology and ecology. They remain, for the large part, unexplored, fostering a pervasive sense of intrigue. With the persistent march of technological progress, it's only a matter of time before these sleeping giants reveal more of their well-guarded secrets. In the meantime, they remain both a testament to the wondrous marvels of our planet and an enduring symbol of our thirst for understanding.

Chapter 5. Vast Valleys: Earth's Enduring Echoes

The deepest crevices, the sinuous gorges, the elongated voids decorating the face of our beloved planet, these are Earth's valleys. An integral part of landforms, these vast structures are primarily sculpted by erosional activities - most notably glacier movements and river actions.

5.1. A Brief Overview of Valleys

Valleys come in all shapes and sizes. There are the V-shaped valleys which are usually carved by rivers and watershed runoff; U-shaped valleys, on the other hand, are typically formed by the glacial activity. Some valleys are wide with gentle slopes, while others are narrow and steep, giving rise to dramatic topography. From the snow-laden valleys of the Himalayas to the verdant gorges of the Amazon, valleys, in their unique ways, provide habitats for a myriad of lifeforms and facilitate vital biogeochemical processes.

5.2. The Birth of a Valley

Let us delve deeper into how these geographical giants come into being. Valleys are commonly birthed through the relentless forces of nature acting over long periods. First off, rivers play a significant role in this process. As rivers meander across the land, they erode the relative lows while leaving the highs untouched. Over time, this differential erosion gives rise to what we call a valley. This erosion occurs not only on the surface but also deep below, eventually leading to a well-carved river valley.

However, not all valleys owe their birth to rivers alone. Some of the most picturesque valleys we see today were once under the firm grip of glaciers during ice ages. These icy invaders sculpted the land by plucking and abrading the rocks beneath, an action that carved out U-shaped valleys which are wider, deeper, and rounder than river valleys.

5.3. Noteworthy Valleys Around the World

Now that we've understood the universal forces at play during the creation of a valley, let's take a trip around the globe and visit some of the most intriguing valleys Earth has to offer.

One of the most well-known valleys on Earth is the Grand Canyon, carved by the Colorado River in the United States. This monumental valley boasts an intricate web of side canyons, cliffs, and ledges that span over 277 miles long and a mile deep. Its raw beauty, highlighted by red-orange hues, is a testament to the power of river erosion over millions of years.

Meanwhile, on the European continent, the Rhône Valley in France stands as a testament to the sculpting power of ice. This U-shaped valley, broad and open, with terraced sides covered with lush vineyards, was brutally carved by glaciers during the last Ice Age. Today, it cradles the river Rhône and flawlessly blends natural beauty with human heritage.

A contrasting landscape can be observed in the Great Rift Valley, stretching from Lebanon in the Middle East to Mozambique in Southeast Africa—a geological wonder that extends more than 4,500 miles. Here, the birth of the valley owes its existence primarily to tectonic activities, as the Arabian and African plates continuously drift apart.

5.4. Valleys as Cradles of Civilization

Historically, valleys have played pivotal roles as cradles of civilization. Their river systems provided primitive cultures with water for irrigation and transportation, fostering agricultural advancements and trade. The fertile banks of the Nile River framed by the Sahara desert, the Tigris and Euphrates Valley, and the Indus Valley have been home to some of the world's oldest and most enduring cultures.

Moreover, valleys serve as bio-corridors, fostering biodiversity and providing habitat for an array of fauna and flora.

5.5. Conservation: A Key Concern

Despite their seeming resilience, valleys are sensitive to environmental and human-induced changes. Climate change impacts, like increased flooding and glacial retreat, can disrupt their delicate ecosystem balance. Additionally, urban development, deforestation, and unsustainable tourism practices often pose threats to these landforms.

Valleys are gateways to our planet's history, holding the narratives of Earth's past deep within their walls. As such, conserving these phenomenal structures is paramount, and sustainably interacting with these landscapes should be the cornerstone of our future explorations. As we journey deeper into the heart of our planet, valleys offer us a window into a world that has been millions of years in the making—a world humming with beauty and echoing with ancient tales.

Today, our exploration concludes in these magical chasms. But the Earth is vast, and there are miles and miles of wonders waiting to be discovered. Let us continue to wander and marvel at the wonders that Mother Earth has curated over millennia. After all, even when we journey deep below our feet, we are merely scratching the surface of the geological splendors that lie hidden, just waiting to tell their extraordinary stories.

Chapter 6. Caves: Inside the Whispering Darkness

In the depths of the earth, beyond the reach of the sun's brilliance, caves lay swathed in an eternal shroud of darkness. These subterranean worlds, characterized by their silence and secrecy, carry an eerie sense of mystery and richness woven into their stone-cored edifice.

6.1. The Birth of a Cave

Creating a cavernous labyrinth beneath the earth's crust takes time measured not in mere centuries, but in hundreds of thousands, or even millions, of years. The mason behind these intriguing landforms is none other than the persistent and patient workings of nature—consistently flowing water, acid rain, and the resolute erosion of softer layers of rock.

Water, permeating the ground, first finds its way into tiny fractures in the rock. The weak carbonic acid formed when rain combines with carbon dioxide in the soil gradually dissolves the limestone or dolomite along these fractures. Over eons, minute pores transform into extensive corridors and chambers, forming the first inklings of a cave.

6.2. Types of Caves

Caves vary tremendously based on the processes that form them, the rock types they are carved from, and the environmental conditions within. Following are some notable types:

Solution caves are the most widespread, usually forming in soluble rocks like limestone, dolomite, and gypsum. They form through the dissolving action of groundwater charged with carbonic acid.

Lava caves, also known as lava tubes, arise from volcanic activity. They occur when the outer layer of a lava flow cools and hardens, while the hot fluid lava underneath continues to flow, ultimately draining away and leaving behind a hollow pipe.

Sea caves are formed from the relentless gnawing of sea waves at softer rocks along the coastline. With the ebb and flow of the tides, the caves continue to deepen, leading to an intricate network of shadowy corridors and ecosystems that vary with the tides.

Glacier caves, born from the interplay of ice and heat, are found within ice and under glaciers. They result from the melting of ice by geothermal heat or the warmer currents of air, leading to strikingly gorgeous formations sculpted in ice.

6.3. The Hidden Climate Archive

Caves harbor treasures of climatic data locked within their intricate mazes. Speleothems—the fascinating structures within caves—are nature's indirect chroniclers of past climate changes. These formations, including stalagmites, stalactites, flowstones, and columns, are formed by the slow drip of mineral-rich water. Each droplet contributes a minuscule layer of calcite, tracing an incremental proxy record over millennia of the climatic conditions during each stage of its growth. Scientists, therefore, often refer to caves as time capsules, making them potent archives of ancient biospheres.

6.4. Cave Ecosystems: Life in the Dark

Contrary to the uninitiated belief, caves are not barren wastelands of darkness. They host complex ecosystems brimming with life forms—many of which have evolved to survive in the permanent absence of light. These remarkable cave-dwellers, or troglobites, have adapted to total darkness, scarcity of food, cold temperatures, and high levels of humidity, yielding a surreal and austere world alive with intrigue and survival.

Striking stalagmite forests, phosphorescent walls brimming with glow worms, swarms of bats clinging to cavern ceilings, blind fish navigating in utmost darkness, and ethereal formations of rock sculptures—these are but a sliver of the incredible life forms and breathtaking scenes within these mysterious geological features.

6.5. Veining the Earth: The World's Longest Caves

Within Earth's crust, an intricate network of caves veins our planet—some so extensive that they dwarf the wildest of imaginations. The Mammoth Cave system in Kentucky, USA, is the longest known cave in the world, stretching over 405 miles. Similarly magnificent, the Sarawak Chamber in Malaysia's Gunung Mulu National Park is the world's most voluminous cave chamber, boasting enough space to accommodate 40 Boeing 747 airplanes.

6.6. Caves: Not Just for Speleologists

Caves are not just scientific curiosities. They serve societal functions too. From being revered as sacred sanctuaries in numerous cultures to being utilized as storage vaults, from offering thrilling adventure tourism opportunities to featuring as film sets, caves are woven into the texture of human existence in multifarious ways.

Their stories, whispered in the echo of dripping water and howled into the void by gusty winds, share the age-old tales of Earth's lifetime. Unchanging yet constantly evolving, silent yet reverberating with whispers of the deep past, caves are as enigmatic as they are enlightening, inviting us, time and again, into the heart of their whispering darkness.

Chapter 7. Islands: The Solitary Outposts of Nature

There's an inherent allure of islands, those tiny specks of land surrounded on all sides by the vast expanses of water. They seem to carry with them a sense of tranquility, solitude, and uniqueness. Yet, far from being tranquil and solitary, islands are tectonic beings, carrying with them tales of Earth's dynamic geological history. From the fiery birth of volcanic islands to the whispered erosion of continental fragments, islands are the solitary outposts of Nature's narrative.

7.1. Birth of an Island

Islands are born in various ways, but volcanic islands are some of the most dramatic in their formation. Born from the fury of Earth's belly, these landforms are a testament to our planet's restless internal heat engine. The process begins thousands of meters below the ocean surface, in the molten heart of Earth where tectonic plates interact.

New earth material is introduced on our planet's surface through volcanic eruptions, both on land and under water. But only those occurring in relatively shallow waters can create islands. The eruption of a submarine volcano can spill out a mound of lava that, over time and multiple eruptions, piles above the ocean surface. Once the tip pierces the ocean's surface, continual deposition of ash and lava helps the island rise and grow.

Hawaii and Iceland, for instance, owe their existence to this fiery process. Hawaii lies in the middle of the Pacific Plate, above a hotspot – a plume of mantle material that rises from the depths of the Earth to puncture the crust and create volcanic activity. Iceland, on the other hand, is located on the Mid-Atlantic Ridge, where the North American and Eurasian plates are drifting apart, creating room for magma from the mantle to rise and form new crust.

7.2. Formation of Coral Islands

When it comes to islands, Mother Nature doesn't just wield fire; she also uses life itself. Coral islands, like those found in the Maldives or the Great Barrier Reef, are formed from the skeletons of tiny marine creatures known as corals.

Coral consist of colonies of tiny animals called polyps which secrete a limestone skeleton. As polyps die, new ones grow on top of the old, creating a mound of skeletons. With the help of wave action, these skeletal mounds grow and take shape into rigid structures called reefs. When coral reefs grow around a volcanic island, an atoll can form. This typically happens when the volcano becomes inactive and starts sinking. As the island submerges, the reef continues to grow upwards, often with a lagoon between the mantle of coral and the disappearing peak of the volcano.

7.3. Continental Islands: Fragments of Landmasses

A third, often less thought-of, category of islands—continental islands— owe their origins to a different sort of geological dynamic. These islands were once part of a larger landmass, but became isolated through the forces of erosion and, more significantly, changes in sea level driven by glaciation cycles.

Great Britain, for instance, was once attached to mainland Europe. During the glaciations, when a significant amount of water was locked up in ice caps, sea levels fell, and the English Channel was dry land. As the ice caps melted in the interglacial periods, sea levels rose once more, isolating Great Britain from the European mainland.

7.4. The Dynamic Lives of Islands

Beyond their creation, islands lead dynamic lives. They grow, evolve, and can even die. They are shaped by the elements—wind, water, and ice. Erosion and weathering, as well as volcanic activity and tectonic shifts, play substantial roles in sculpting these landforms over time.

Islands also play host to a unique blend of life. Isolated from mainland influences, they are hotspots for endemism, or species that can only be found in a single location. This has resulted in a wide variety of wildlife and vegetation that adds another layer to their geological narrative.

By studying these solitary outposts of Nature, we don't just learn about earth material, tectonics, and life; we also gain a profound understanding of the planet's intricacies. Each island, with its unique formation and life history, provides pieces of a large, intricate puzzle that constitutes our understanding of Earth's geological history. Every grain of sand and every pebble on an island beach carries an untold story—of violent eruptions, of quiet coral growth, of ice caps growing and shrinking and of millennia-long weathering—that awaits discovery.

The beauty of islands is not merely in their isolated solitude, far-flung on the planet's oceans; it lies in the silent tales they tell about Earth's past and present. It is this that makes the study of islands truly a journey into the wonders of our dynamic planet. So, as we wrap up this chapter and look to the subsequent chapters, we continue on this thrill of discovery, exploring the sleeping giants and their varied, impressive and ever-intriguing tales.

Chapter 8. Volcanoes: Fountains of Fiery Majesty

From the dawn of human memory, volcanoes have imbued us with a sense of awe and fear. These majestic mountains that spew forth fire and cobblestones of molten rock upon the earth are as deadly as they are beautiful, and they serve as powerful reminders of the geothermal activity brewing beneath our feet.

8.1. Underlying Mechanics of Volcanoes

Understanding the jaw-dropping spectacle of a volcanic eruption begins with peering deep into the earth's crust. At this subterranean level, our planet is a quarry of churning and rumbling forces. Astoundingly hot molten rock—or magma—exists under tremendous pressure. When this pressure becomes too great, the magma seeks release at the surface through weaknesses in the earth's crust, spawning the awe-inspiring spectacle we know as a volcanic eruption.

Volcanoes aren't choosy about where they occur. They spring to life along fault lines, underwater in the ocean's mysterious depths, and even under thick glaciers. Their formation has shaped and continues to mold our planet's geology, influencing ecosystems and weather patterns and ultimately playing an integral role in the evolution and adaptability of life on Earth.

8.2. Different Types of Volcanoes

Volcanology, the study of volcanoes and volcanic phenomena, has revealed much about these geological anomalies, including the fact that not all volcanoes are created equal. Volcanologists classify volcanoes into several types: shield volcanoes, composite volcanoes (also known as stratovolcanoes), cinder cones, and lava domes.

Shield volcanoes, like those found in Hawaii, are broad, domed volcanoes with long, sloping sides created by highly fluid low-viscosity lava eruptions. Composite volcanoes—like Mount Fuji in Japan and Mount St. Helens in the U.S.—are typically cone-shaped with steeper slopes, formed by explosive eruptions of viscous, high-gas-content magma, and lesser eruptions of more fluid lava.

Cinder cone volcanoes, the simplest type, build up around a single vent as chunks of magma are blown out, cooling and plunging back to the earth as a cinder that eventually forms the cone. Lastly, lava dome volcanoes are created when highly viscous lava is pushed out from the vent and piles up around it. Instead of flowing away, it squeezes out like toothpaste and hardens, creating a mound.

8.3. The Explosive Power of Volcanoes

The heart-quickening spectacle of a volcanic eruption is an unfiltered display of our planet's raw power. The quantity of material expelled and the force behind it can be truly colossal. Take for instance the 1883 eruption of Krakatoa in Indonesia. Heard over 2,000 miles away, it remains one of the world's most devastating volcanic eruptions. At its peak, the noise generated by the eruption was reckoned to be the loudest sound ever heard in modern history.

Volcanic gas clouds, ash fall, pyroclastic flows, and lahars (volcanic mudflows) have the capacity not only to wipe towns off the map but to reshape the entire landscape. Ash thrown up to altitudes of over 32 kilometers can have a global impact on climate. For instance, the eruption of Tambora in 1815 released so much gas and ash into the atmosphere that it lowered average global temperatures, resulting in the infamous "Year without a Summer" in 1816.

8.4. Volcanoes: A Source of Life?

Though it seems paradoxical, the same violent eruptions that cause mass destruction also sow the seeds of life—quite literally. Volcanic soils are among the most fertile on Earth. The nutrient-rich ash and rock fragments that volcanoes spew forth feed the earth, enabling the lush growth of vegetation.

Islands formed from volcanic activity, like the Galapagos, are stark evidence of this life-giving capacity. Over time, these islands develop rich, unique biodiversity—a testament to the unlikely, life-nurturing byproducts of these fiery mountains.

Furthermore, the deep-sea vents volcanoes produce support a myriad of marine life forms. These extremophile organisms have adapted to their home's harsh conditions, giving scientists new insights into the bounds of life on Earth and potentially other planets.

8.5. Living with Volcanoes

Humans have a long history of living with volcanoes. From the ancient settlements of Pompeii and Herculaneum—tragically lost in AD 79 to the eruption of Mount Vesuvius—to the modern cities nestled beside active volcanoes, such as Naples (Italy) and Kagoshima (Japan), we have continuously been drawn to these compelling and fertile regions.

The hazards are ever-present, but so too are the benefits. Volcanic areas are not only rich in soils but also natural geothermal energy. Countries like Iceland and New Zealand harness this energy, thus reducing their reliance on fossil fuels.

Volcanoes, in their fearsome majesty, are a fascinating blend of destructive and creative energy. Studying these windows to Earth's fiery heart provides incredible insight into our dynamic planet's formation, operation, and even pointers to the origins and longevity of life itself. Mankind's relationship with volcanoes is typified by an inquisitive fascination—with every eruption, we edge slightly closer to understanding these fountains of fiery majesty.

Chapter 9. Earthquakes and Fault Lines: A Planet in Motion

In the heartlands of our planet, continental plates shift, collide, and grind against each other in an age-old dance choreographed by the indifferent forces of nature. The effects of these movements ripple outwards in waves of energy, causing one of the most fearsome and awe-inspiring phenomena we know—an earthquake.

Unseen and often unexpected, these subterranean forces shape Earth, creating and modifying her landscapes over geological timescales. They trigger the birth of mountains, the formation of valleys, and can reconfigure an entire region in a matter of minutes. Interlocking in a delicate equilibrium, earthquakes and fault lines provide invaluable insights into our planet's dynamic persona.

9.1. Understanding Earthquakes

To understand earthquakes, one must first grasp the fundamental premise of plate tectonics. Earth's lithosphere, the hard outer shell, isn't a single, continuous piece. Rather, it's composed of a mosaic of slabs or "plates" floating atop the semi-fluid layer called the asthenosphere.

As the plates move under the influence of heat convection currents, they interact at their boundaries. Divergent boundaries, where plates move apart, create spaces for molten material to rise and solidify, forming new crust. On the other hand, convergent boundaries, where plates crash into each other, result in one plate beneath the other—a process known as subduction—which can cause volcanic activities. Lastly, we have transform boundaries, where plates slide past each other horizontally.

Most earthquakes are born along these restless plate boundaries, primarily as a result of the immense pressure and strain accumulated during these interactions. When the stress overcomes the rock material's inherent resistance, it's released in sudden bursts of energy, causing seismic waves that propagate through the Earth's crust—an event we perceive as an earthquake.

9.2. The Anatomy of a Fault Line

Fault lines are the visible scars of these seismic disturbances, embodying the literal breakpoint where rocks have slipped due to tectonic forces. Even though the terms "fault" and "fault line" are used interchangeably, a fault refers to a fracture or zone of fractures between two blocks of rock, while a fault line is the planar feature that represents the surface trace of a fault.

Faults can be classified into three primary types based on the movement of the blocks:

1. Normal Faults: The block above the fault plane, also called the hanging wall, moves downwards relative to the lower block or footwall—usually seen at divergent boundaries.

2. Reverse Faults: An inverse of a normal fault, the hanging wall is pushed upwards relative to the footwall. Reverse faults are common at convergent boundaries.

3. Strike-slip Faults: The blocks move horizontally past each other. These faults often follow transform boundaries, such as the notorious San Andreas Fault.

The length of a fault line can range from less than a meter to hundreds of kilometers, but it's not always the size that counts. Sometimes, smaller faults can produce sizable earthquakes if the slippage or strain released is significant enough.

9.3. Recording and Measuring Earthquakes

The study of earthquakes—seismology—relies extensively on the data collected from seismographs, instruments that record a seismic wave's arrival time, amplitude, and frequency. By recording seismic activities from several locations globally, scientists triangulate the source of an earthquake, also called the epicenter, and its depth (focal depth).

The magnitude of an earthquake, a measure of the energy released at the source, is quantified on the Richter Scale through logarithmic calculations. However, modern scientists prefer the moment magnitude scale (Mw) as it accommodates higher ranges and provides more accurate readings for larger quakes. The perceived intensity of an earthquake is measured on the Modified Mercalli Index, which is dependent on the area's demographics, local building conditions, and distance from the epicenter.

9.4. Earthquake Prediction and Safety Measures

Efforts to predict earthquakes have been a primary focus of seismology. Although we have made great strides in understanding why and how earthquakes happen, forecasting them with pinpoint accuracy remains an elusive goal. Nonetheless, hazard assessment maps and studies of fault line histories have proven valuable in designating high-risk areas and establishing building codes to safeguard human lives.

During an earthquake, safety is paramount. "Drop, Cover, and Hold On" is widely propagated as the safest response. Furthermore, construction standards that boost structural integrity in earthquake-prone zones are crucial. Early warning systems, although providing a minimal lead-time, are effective in alerting local population and initiating automatic safeguards in critical infrastructure.

Earthquakes and fault lines stand as a humbling reminder of our planet's ceaseless dynamism. As we delve deeper into their mysteries, we equip ourselves with the knowledge to coexist with these terrestrial titans, emblems of a planet eternally in motion. As we conclude this chapter, remember, an earthquake is not the planet's wrath, but a testament to its ceaseless labor in the forge of geology, punctuating epochs in Earth's enduring saga.

Chapter 10. Glaciers and Icefields: The Frozen Frontier

Our adventure begins with a journey through glaciers and icefields, those ethereal stretches of frozen terrain, marred by millennia of slow, churning movement. Time and scale take on new meaning when one grapples with these icy leviathans, perhaps most aptly characterized as rivers of ice.

10.1. The Making of a Glacier

Understanding glaciers begins with the concept of the snow line - the lofty altitude in mountainous regions above which snowfall does not melt seasonally and accumulates year after year. Over ages, the eerie silence of these desolate zones is pierced only by the unique crunch of imprinted layer upon layer of snow.

Under its own weight, the granular snow gradually compacts into a solid mass, the blue tint indicative of its dense structure that absorbs and refracts light differently. Known as firn, it's an intermediate stage frozen in time, destined to transition into the fascinating formations we call glaciers.

The birth of a glacier is a grand spectacle, a testament to the immense pressures our planet can exert. The lower layers of firn are subjected to such massive pressure they fuse into an enormous mass of natural ice. This rate of compaction varies based on altitude, climate, and snow availability. The relentless dance of precipitation and pressure creates glaciers, often taking up to a hundred years!

Once formed, glaciers continue to shape our landscapes through two opposing processes - accumulation and ablation. Accumulation refers to the constant supply of new ice through snowfall, while ablation signifies the natural melting, calving, or sublimation of ice.

Although they appear stationary, glaciers are anything but. Creeping downhill at rates ranging from a few millimeters to several meters per day, the glaciers carve their path with a might that's hard to fathom until one witnesses the aftermath. This process of glacial movement, fittingly termed glacial flow, transforms coarse mountainous profiles into elegantly sculpted valleys.

10.2. Glacial Landforms and Features: Nature's Ice Sculptures

As they crawl along their path, glaciers remodel the landscape in their reflection, creating unique topographical features along the way. Amongst these are the textbook U-shaped valleys, characterized by steep sides and often flat valley floors, a stark change from the V-shaped valleys commonly formed by rivers.

Similarly, cirques or cwm, another impressive formation, represent an amphitheater-shaped hollow scooped out at the mountain peak. When multiple cirques erode a mountain, the resulting knife-like ridges are known as arêtes. If the process continues, it gives rise to pyramidal peaks, isolated and daunting.

At a larger scale, glacial ice sheets completely transform continental landscapes. Retreating ice sheets leave behind drumlins, streamlined, elongated hills formed under the ice. These drumlins can often occur in vast swarms, beautifully showcasing the direction of glacial movement.

The icy behemoth leaves more subtle signatures as well. Striations or grooves found on exposed bedrock speak of glacial abrasion, a mechanical grinding symbolizing the glacier's once towering presence.

10.3. The Earth's Living Glaciers

There exist today, across the populated world, numerous regions where glaciers continue to shape the landscape. Atop the list is the Antarctic ice sheet, the planet's largest glacial body covering approximately 98% of the continent. Its effect on global sea levels and climate patterns is as colossal as the ice sheet itself.

Greenland follows suit with the second-largest ice sheet. Standouts also include the glaciers of Patagonia in South America, covering a sizable portion of the renowned Andes mountain range, and the glacial regions spanning the Rockies, the Himalayas, and the Alps.

Take, for instance, the illustrious Perito Moreno Glacier in Argentine Patagonia. One of the few advancing glaciers worldwide, it periodically ruptures in a fascinating display of the sheer might of nature.

10.4. The Uneroded Legacy

Glaciers and icefields have sculpted the world we know and continue to do so while also serving as crucial freshwater reserves. Their study grants us invaluable insights into our planet's climate history and predictions for the future. Yet, these ancient giants are at risk. Global warming is causing a rapid retreat of glaciers worldwide, and the day isn't far when some might be relegated to just the pages of nature's history.

Few things remind us of the ephemerality and resilience of our planet as profoundly as glaciers. They are magnificent, relentless, and, most importantly, keepers of Earth's oldest secrets. Our Frozen Frontier beckons you to respect and appreciate it, for in its icy expanses lie the stories of our past and the keys to our future.

Chapter 11. Toward the Future: Preservation and Impact of Geological Anomalies

Understanding our planet's geological anomalies is not just an exercise of academic curiosity; it's a commitment to preserving our Earth for future generations. As we venture toward the future, the impact and preservation of these remarkable formations take on heightened significance.

11.1. THE INTRICATE BALANCE OF NATURE

Geological anomalies shape nature's balance in ways subtler than one might realize. Besides their visual charm and natural significance, these phenomena play pivotal roles in biodiversity, climate patterns, and even human life. Their influence extends beyond their physical boundaries, affecting local and global environments.

Mountains, for instance, drive weather patterns by influencing air circulation. They also serve as homes to diverse flora and fauna, some of which exist nowhere else on the planet. Similarly, caves harbor unique ecosystems, providing shelter for species adapted to the extreme conditions found within their dark depths.

By better understanding these anomalies, we gain insight into the intricate interconnections between our planet's geological and biological spheres. Every deviation, tremor, and shift has a ripple effect through Earth's complex ecosystems. In this delicate equilibrium, preservation becomes paramount.

11.2. MAN'S IMPACT ON GEOLOGICAL ANOMALIES

Humans have left an indelible mark on our planet's landscapes. Industrialization, urbanization, mining—these activities have altered natural terrains, often irreversibly. Through human activity, we are not just transforming geological anomalies but threatening their very existence.

This degradation impacts biodiversity, risking the extinction of numerous specialist species unable to adapt to rapid environmental changes. It also has dire implications for humanity, especially for communities directly reliant on these geological structures.

Our actions today connote profound consequences for generations to come. Therefore, assessing and mitigating our influence is pivotal; by recognizing our past mistakes, we can design a future where cohabitation with nature attends mutual respect and understanding.

11.3. THE ROLE OF SCIENCE AND TECHNOLOGY

The tide might seem relentless, but science and technology offer light at the end of the tunnel. Utilizing cutting-edge techniques, researchers capture invaluable data from geological anomalies—data critical to understanding our planet's past and predicting its future.

One such method is Remote Sensing, empowers us with the ability to observe, monitor, and analyze the Earth's geological formations from a distance. This technology plays an integral role in collecting extensive information, aiding research on climate change, geological disruptions, and their overall impact on biodiversity.

Additionally, we see advancements in Virtual and Augmented Reality creating virtual tours, thereby reducing the ecological footprint of tourism. This facilitates broad accessibility and education on geological wonders without their physical disturbance.

11.4. PRESERVATION FOR THE FUTURE: A RESPONSIBILITY WE SHARE

The responsibility of preserving these mystical wonders transcends borders and generations. It's a global challenge that necessitates collective engagement and swift action.

Conservation efforts work to promote biodiversity, protect endangered species, and reduce the impact of human activities. National parks, wildlife reserves, and UNESCO World Heritage Sites highlight these endeavors, safeguarding the Earth's most precious geological anomalies.

Additionally, community-driven initiatives play an instrumental role in these efforts. In numerous locations worldwide, local residents have become custodians of their surrounding geological wonders. They work tirelessly, often in collaboration with global organizations, to conserve and sustainably manage these areas.

11.5. EMBRACING THE FUTURE

As we stride toward the future, we must learn not only to live with these anomalies but also to thrive with them. Investing in education, supporting effective policies, and embracing sustainable practices are critical steps in this direction. By making informed choices, we contribute to a sustainable future where both natural wonders and human cultures co-exist harmoniously.

Humans may be the Earth's greatest geologic force, but we have the potential to be its greatest protector. Today's actions shape tomorrow's world. Let us pledge to leave behind a rich, diverse, and beautiful planet for the countless generations awaiting their turn to revel in Earth's tapestry of geological anomalies.

In this complex dance between preservation and progress, we play a defining role. The geological anomalies we marvel at are not just nature's sculptures; they are poignant reminders of our responsibility as Earth's custodians. It's these Sleeping Giants' stories we carry forward, written not just in the language of science but in the human story of discovery, respect, and preservation. Thus, let's cherish and nurture these narratives, for they spotlight the path toward a future shared in sustainable harmony with our planet.

www.ingramcontent.com/pod-product-compliance
Lightning Source LLC
Chambersburg PA
CBHW071048260726